MW01064788

Other Books by Patrick Ellam

Sopranino

The Sportsman's Guide to the Caribbean

Wind Song

Yacht Cruising

THINGS I REMEMBER

by

Patrick Ellam

iUniverse, Inc.
New York Bloomington

Things I Remember

iUniverse books may be ordered through booksellers or by contacting:

iUniverse
1663 Liberty Drive
Bloomington, IN 47403
www.iuniverse.com
1-800-Authors (1-800-288-4677)

ISBN: 978-1-4502-1257-1 (pbk)

Printed in the United States of America

iUniverse rev. date: 4/28/10

CONTENTS

1 . Grandfather's House 9

2 . Down to the Sea 18

3 . Maidenhead 29

4 . Up in the Mountains 37

5 . Norway & Sweden 46

6 . Defending London 54

7 . Le Havre & St Nazaire 60

8 . The Battle of Britain 67

9 . A Hundred Women 78

10 . Spy School 89

11 . Special Operations 99

12 . Wartime London 110

13 . The Swiss Border 116

14 . Ceylon & Singapore 126

What Happened Next 133

1. GRANDFATHER'S HOUSE

It must have been 1925 because I was five years old. All the family was at my grandfather's house for Christmas, standing in a circle in the living room. And in the middle was a child's car, with a seat and a steering wheel and pedals to make it go. They were looking at me, encouraging me to get in it, but I knew what to do, because I had seen my daddy play with his car many times. I laid down on the floor, put my face under the front of it, and shouted "Damn and blast this bloody car".

The grownups were not surprised. Cars were not reliable in those days - you often had to fix the engine at the side of the road - and I sounded just like Daddy. So they laughed and went on talking to each other, while I left and pedalled my car down a path to the end of the garden.

The house was in Sidcup, a suburb of London, and I liked to stay there because interesting things happened. One day, my grandfather decided to clean the chimney over the big fireplace in the living room. He put a blank cartridge in a pistol, stuck it up the chimney as far as he could reach and fired. There was a bang, then a swoosh and half a ton of black soot came down on top of him, leaving only his eyes showing.

For years my grandmother had complained to him that the drawer where she kept her sewing things was hard to open. It was waist high in a big chest in the dining room and to open it she would put a foot up on the chest beside it and pull as hard as she could. She was a big, heavy woman but that would only open it about a foot and she had to reach inside for her things.

But one day my grandfather took the drawer out, planed it down and lubricated it, so that it would open smoothly with no effort at all. Then my grandmother came to get something, put her foot on the chest, gave a great heave and went several feet through the air before landing on her back on the floor, while her things went flying through the air like shrapnel.

He made up for it by building her a summer house, big enough to play bridge in with her friends, mounted on a turntable. It was open on one side and when she wanted more sun or more shade, she would step out and turn it the right way.

Another time, a man came to read a meter in the basement, so my grandmother opened a door at the top of a steep flight of stairs, said "Step this way" and went smartly down to the bottom on her back-side. To which the man replied "I'd rather not, madam" and went down to help her.

She was deaf and had an ear trumpet, a black tube about four feet long, two or three inches wide at one end, tapering down to a small earpiece at the other. To speak to her, you waved to get her attention, then spoke into the wide end. But she was good at lip reading and, sitting in the front window of her house, she could tell you what people were saying to each other at the bus stop across the street.

Cars did not have electric starters yet. You started them by turning a handle at the front. My grandfather had a big car and it took all his strength to turn the handle, so he stood with his feet wide apart. And once he left it in gear. When he turned the handle, the engine fired once and stopped, making the car go forward and pin his feet down with the two front wheels. And it was a while before we heard him shouting for help.

One day my uncle Tom came by on his motorcycle, tall and handsome with his monocle and cigarette holder, and found me building a sled. But it was not winter yet, so I said I needed some snow. And he said "You're too young for cocaine".

Drugs were not illegal at that time. People could buy any they wanted in a store and it was not a problem. A few people used them but there was no great profit to be made on them, so nobody made any effort to get people hooked.

At dinner one evening, I was having trouble cutting a piece of meat and my grandfather told me to move the knife forward and backward, like a saw. That didn't make sense to me, since there were no teeth on the knife, but I did and it worked.

He was a lawyer and his brother invented a copying machine called the Ellams Duplicator. The first one was on display in the Science Museum in London. From that he built up a business with three factories, thirty five offices in England and branches all over the world, selling office equipment and supplies. And at 70 he retired, leaving his two sons to run it.

My father was the older one and he looked after the factories and offices in England, while his brother went around the world every three years, visiting the foreign branches. The head office was in London and we lived in Maidenhead, about 30 miles to the west of there, on the banks of the River Thames.

My mother had the knack of foreseeing things. One day she was supposed to take a train to London and meet my father, go to a party and come back in his car. But by mid morning she had a strong premonition that something awful was going to happen, so she called him on the phone and didn't go.

Coming back late at night, my father skidded on a patch of ice and his sports car rolled over. With nobody in the passenger's seat, he was thrown clear and survived. But if she had been with him, they would both have been trapped in the car and killed.

She had her own way of thinking, too. If we were in a car and came to a crossroads and she said "Go straight on" that did not mean we should go straight ahead, it meant we should go the way she usually went.

She was concerned about her appearance, about always being well dressed and 'turned out', whatever that meant.

One day she was walking across the vast paved area inside a London railroad station when her silk panties fell down, so she stepped out of them and kept on walking, holding my hand tightly and looking straight ahead, while I called out "Mummy, Mummy, look! Your panties fell down" pointing back with one hand while she dragged my sideways by the other.

Though I was an only child, there was plenty of company at home. We had a cook, two maids and a gardener, who also polished the shoes, the brass and the silverware. The policeman came by each day and the cook kept his favorite kind of beer handy. There were some boys who lived nearby. So there was no lack of interesting things to do.

Once a week, a man came down the road with a barrow full of turtles and an old lady nearby had one as a pet. So we took hers, when she wasn't looking, and exchanged it for a slightly smaller one, each week. Soon she was convinced that her turtle was wasting away, so she fed it all kinds of food but nothing seemed to help until we started exchanging it for a larger one. Then it started getting too large, until we ran out of money.

Outside a nearby pub there was a machine that sold a pack of cigarettes for a shilling, a coin about the size of a quarter. So the older boys made round pieces of ice in a refrigerator (using a mold slightly larger, to allow for melting) put them in it and sold the cigarettes at half price to people coming out. The nice thing was that any evidence soon melted.

I had a mongrel dog called Bonzo who fetched golf balls. We would go to a golf course with a bucket and soon we would have plenty of balls to sell. But he would not wait for a ball to stop rolling before he picked it up, which was embarrasing.

Once I took him to a seaside resort and as I was walking along a beach with a friend, we passed a woman in a bare backed swimsuit, sitting on the sand, facing the sea. Bonzo was behind us and when he got to her, he relieved himself down her back. She made quite a fuss and it was hard for us to convince people that Bonzo was no friend of ours, though he wasn't then.

My father made a door opener before they were heard of. His garage had two doors that swung outward, so he put springs on them, to make them open, and a latch over the middle, to hold them shut. Then he strung a steel guitar string horizontally, above them, and tuned it to the sound of his car's horn. When he blew his horn, the guitar string vibrated, touched a contact and made an electric magnet pull up a latch in the middle. Then both doors were swung wide open by their springs.

It worked well but if anyone in a car with a horn of the same frequency as his happened to blow it as he passed our house, the garage doors would swing open.

Another time he bought a yellow car and decided to paint it black. So he got a spray gun, taped over the shiny parts and painted one side. Then he got bored and left it that way, with one side yellow and the other side black, which confused people who saw him go down a street and come back in what looked like an identical car but of a different color.

I was only allowed to have five ideas a day and one of them was a board with four wheels of the same size, in which the front and back axles were connected by a chain, with a small sprocket on one axle and a large sprocket on the other. If you pushed it forward, the large sprocket would turn once, then the chain would make the small one turn twice. Then the big one would turn twice and the small one would turn four times. So the board would go faster and faster, for ever. But it didn't work.

Our house was beside the Thames and almost every year the river would flood for a few days. Then the water would be a foot deep in the living room, so my mother had the servants take the furniture upstairs and my father caught a ride to higher ground each morning on a horse drawn milk wagon that looked just like a chariot but with huge, shiny cans standing on it.

When the flood ended, the brown, muddy water of the river would drain through the carpet like a seive and leave behind an inch or so of fine potting soil for the gardener. And there was always a line around the living room walls, that was shown with pride to visitors from dryer places.

In nice weather we often went out on the water and my father promised to give me a boat when I could swim across the river with my clothes and shoes on. There was a strong current at that point but at seven I passed the test.

2. DOWN TO THE SEA

Every summer we went to Itchenor, a village on a river that ran down to the sea on the south coast of England. My father and his brother both had yachts that they kept there.

Father's first one that I remember was Wendy, a 30 foot gaff rigged cutter. Then came Pipefish, a 40 foot power boat that was haunted by her previous owner, the Reverend H. F. Speed, who died aboard her. Each evening when we were in the cabin finishing our dinner, the doors would swing open as he came in. But he didn't do anything and eventually we got used to him.

Usually we would drive from London on a Saturday and take the boat down the river on Sunday, anchor off a beach, go ashore in a dinghy and catch shrimp with nets on poles, that we pushed along in a foot or so of water. There was no way to get there by land, so the people all came in their own boats but on a fine Sunday there were many, of all sizes.

Then came Melissa, an 84 foot twin engined power boat, with a full time engineer and steward, that was rather big for trips down to the harbor mouth but good for entertaining the actors and actresses Father met in London. One day there was an explosion in the engine room and he shouted down the funnel "Pat! Whatever you're doing, Stop it!"

The wooden hull was built in Canada. During the first world war, the British ordered sixty of them but someone made a mistake and they built six hundred, so there were plenty available. They were called ML's (motor launches) and made fine yachts,

With Melissa to live on, my mother and I could stay there all week and I got my first boat, a 9 foot, double ended dinghy, built with overlapping wood strakes. The first year, my father gave me the oars, so I got plenty of practice rowing around the harbor. Then the next year he gave me the mast, rudder and sail, and I spent days and weeks exploring the lonely creeks and marshes.

My boat was called Willie Wet Pants because you had to sit on the floor, for your head to clear the boom, and being quite old, she leaked. But she sailed well with her gaff rig and I learned a great deal about wind and tides.

Later I was allowed to run a larger sailing dinghy that was used to take people from Melissa to and from the dock, about a mile down the river. It was the only way to get there - we had no motor boat - and when a strong current was running, it took skill to dodge between the anchored yachts, while hanging out over the side to prevent her from capsizing and assuring nervous passengers that she wouldn't sink.

Eventually I was so used to that dinghy that I could lower and secure the sail while approaching the dock, take the rudder off, raise the centerboard, step ashore when she arrived and toss a line over a bollard as I walked away.

The summer holidays lasted three months, then it was school the rest of the year, with a holiday at Christmas. The first school I remember was Stubbington in Hampshire, where boys who had done something wrong were laid across the vaulting horse, held by hands and feet, and beaten with a cane by the Sergeant, while the rest of us were made to stand and watch, every Saturday.

There was one good moment in those years. On a visiting day - when parents were allowed to come - there was a fireworks display and at the end, several big rockets on a frame were meant to go up into the dark sky together. But after the fuse was lit, the frame slowly tilted toward the audience. The parents got off the benches and threw themselves on the ground, as the rockets went hissing and sparking, low over their heads.

And we had fun with little things, like asking people to sing the Siamese National Anthem, that we told them started with "Oh wah tah nah Siam".

My other school was Stowe, in the old palace of the Duke of Buckingham. The main building was large - Buckingham Palace in London was the Duke's town place - and we were required to have bicycles to get from one class to another. Once a year the local fox hunt started there and about 300 boys followed it on their bicycles, throwing them over any hedges or streams they came to and scrambling after them, which was fun.

The grounds were vast and the main reason I was sent there was that it had a lake big enough for sailboat races. But at one point it was relatively narrow, with a low wooden dock going out from the shore, its end a hundred yards or so from the far bank. And behind the dock was a path leading up a slope.

One day a new boy showed up with a fine bicycle, so we told him that if he started at the top of the slope and got up enough speed, he could go down the dock and across the lake to the far side without sinking. And he almost made it. He was pedalling furiously, in a cloud of spray, when he sank.

There was a paved road from Stowe to the town of Buckingham, with two rows of huge oak trees on either side of it , set back beyond wide areas of grass. The road went straight, all the way, over hills and valleys, and there was a triumphal arch at the top of one hill, such as you see in cities.

Sometimes on a Sunday, when we had a few hours of freedom, we would go to Buckingham on our bicycles and on one occasion we met a senior boy who invited us to a coffee shop, ordered four cups of coffee and four pieces of cake, took two of each for himself and gave us the others, which we appreciated.

Christopher Milne, whose father wrote Winnie the Pooh, was there and about 300 boys taunted him each time the song 'Christopher Robin is saying his prayers' came over the radio, which must have been quite a hard thing to put up with.

By the way: One of Churchill's people wrote that he should not end a sentence with a preposition and he wrote back 'That is a piece of pedantry, up with which I will not put'.

My mother insisted that I take piano lessons, which were a total failure, year after year. But when I was very much older I started playing Spanish music on a guitar and it was fine.

We had a French master who spoke no English, though he understood it, and our English master left suddenly.

He came into class one day, with two red setters and a 12 gauge shot gun, stood in front of us, looking from side to side across the class, and said "I'm sick and tired of teaching you bourgeois little bastards. I'm going to be a writer." He swept out, followed by his dogs, and never came back.

His name was T. H. White and he wrote a

book called 'A Once and Future King' which became the basis for the Camelot stories in the days when John F. Kennedy was President of the United States.

The classes in carpentry and metal work were interesting. I built a scale model of a ship's cannon about 16 inches long in solid brass. It took several days to drill the hole down the middle of it, which was an inch in diameter, and it was mounted on a low, wide carriage as they were in real life. The high, narrow ones you see would fall over in a seaway.

Then I found some blasting powder in a nearby quarry, to try it out. It would throw a one inch lead ball about 600 feet or you could load it with shot and blast a hole in a hedge. Somehow a master heard of it. He sent for me and said "I hear you have a gun" so I said "Yes, sir" and he said "Bring it here".

I put in a good charge of powder, with some wadding to hold it but no ball or shot, took it to his room and set it in front of the coal fire, that was burning brightly. Then he said "Is it loaded?" and I said "Yes, sir" and he said "Unload it at once" so I tipped the powder out of it but it didn't go off and he swept it up, muttering something I didn't understand.

Other boys found interesting things to do, too. They had been told that methane was inflammable and wondered if a fart would burn, so one night in a dormitory they lit a candle and held it close behind a boy, who obliged them. But they didn't know that methane might explode. There was a bang and a yellow flame, that settled the matter but made him quite sore.

I found cricket very boring. You stood for hours in a field until suddenly a ball went by and people complained because you didn't stop it. But we had fun. We hooked an old Ford spark coil up to the metal trough used as a urinal in a hut by the field, so that a stream of water coming down would conduct electricity at high voltage up to the user. Then we put out rumors about venereal diseases that created satisfactory lines at the doctor's office.

My happiest memory of that school was the day they had a parade for the Officers' Training Corps. Hundreds of parents were there, with flags waving and bands playing, as the boys marched past a huge statue of a man on a horse, rearing up, and a general stood in front of it, returning their salute.

The base was about fifteen feet high and the horse on top of it was bigger than that. So the night before the parade, we made a hole in the top of the horse, which was hollow, put in some water, made a hole in the obvious place under the horse and put a cork in it, with a thread hanging down beside the base.

The next day, as the parade went by, a group of us stood round the base of the statue, someone pulled the thread and the horse pissed on the general. The boys went on marching, the band went on playing, the general stepped aside and went on saluting, while everyone else did their best to ignore it.

That summer, my father and his brother each had a cottage at Itchenor. On a Monday morning, they would drive up to London in one of their cars, the passenger blowing a razzer - a rubber tube with a wooden mouthpiece, that made a farting noise - to see how many people he could make turn round. Beavers (men with beards) were worth two points and a man who fell off his bicycle when he heard the noise gave the player three.

They would get to the office about midday, stay the night in London and work until noon on Tuesday, when they would drive back to Itchenor. Wednesdays they took off, and on Thursday and Friday they did the same thing, each week.

They both had Bentleys in Englsh Racing Green, with tool boxes and batteries on long fenders that swept up from near the driver, over the front wheels, and a spare wheel mounted beside a bonnet with leather straps over it, two huge headlights and a windshield you could open to see through if it got dirty because there were no wipers at that time.

Mr. Bentley complained that the brakes on Bugattis were no good but Sr. Bugatti said "I make cars to go, not to stop" and "Mr. Bentley makes the fastest trucks in the world."

My father had a six liter Bentley saloon for a while but it was so heavy that the tires were smoking after a 30 mile run at high speed. His Rolls Royce was more fun because it had a window you could wind up between the front seats and the back ones, so that the gardener could dress up as a chauffeur. But when the XK 100 Jaguars came along, he stuck to those.

In the cottage one evening I was in bed when an old aunt came up to kiss me good night, which I didn't like, so I raised my knees to lift the blanket, made a bad smell and lowered my knees as she leaned over me, sending a waft of foul air up around my neck, as I smiled innocently and thanked her politely. She reeled back, stared at me, almost certain that I had done it on purpose, and went clomping back down the stairs.

3 . MAIDENHEAD

At home in Maidenhead, my father bought a rubber swimming pool, about 15 feet across and four feet high, that he put on a lawn in the garden. It took three days to fill it with a hose, by which time no one on the street was getting much water, and he set up a diving board, with its end over the middle.

Then he gave a party, invited lots of people, and they were all standing around drinking, while an actor made the first dive. He ran down the springboard, leapt up and spread his arms. His expression changed as he passed over the far side of the pool and landed on his belly on the grass. Then they moved the springboard back, so that its end was before the pool, and others tried it.

We boys found new things to do. The horse drawn milk cart, that came by each day, had been replaced by an electric one that the driver didn't like, because it didn't have the sense to stop at the right houses or move on as he walked from one to another, as the horse used to do. But we obliged him by putting a brick in front of a rear wheel. When he depressed the accelerator pedal, it compressed a spring that moved an arm over a set of contacts, increasing the current to the motor. With the brick there, the cart didn't move while the current built up, then suddenly it leapt forward in a great bound, scattering milk bottles far and wide, which was quite theatrical.

My mother took me to a cupboard where the drinks were kept and let me taste them. There was gin, vermouth, rum, whisky and brandy but they all tasted horrible to me and I didn't bother to try any of them again, for several years. But we put some gin in the bird bath, which had interesting effects.

I have seen sparrows landing with their legs up, sparrows making left turns while banked to the right, sparrows stalling in mid air or missing a branch by a foot, clearly expressing their frustration, for they are cocky about their flying.

The British post office would deliver a

letter with no stamp on it but charge the recipient two pennies instead of one, that was the ordinary rate. So we would mail envelopes to people with notes inside them, saying `Ha Ha Ha, He He He, Tuppence to pay and nothing to see'. Perhaps we were tiresome.

One day we found a man standing outside a shop, reading a newspaper. So we took a large piece of waste paper, lit it and held it a foot or so behind his paper. When he saw the flames shoot up, he crushed his paper into a ball and stamped on it.

The Steam Packet Company ran ferries, called packet boats, between England and France, so we called them on the phone and asked to speak to the managing director. It took us days of persistent calling to reach him but finally he asked what we wanted and we said "What would your price be for a packet of steam?"

Telephones were common by then but radio, that was called `wireless' had just come in. My father had to rig a long wire antenna in the garden and lead it into the house to a `crystal set', a simple receiver with a pair of headphones and a crystal against which you had to put a bit of wire called a `cat's whisker',and find a good place on it. If you were lucky, you would hear "London calling. This is 2LO" and maybe a faint, squeaky violin playing. To let two people hear it at the same time, you put the headphones in a bowl and each put an ear close to it.

There were dinner parties at our house twice a week, with everyone in evening dress, my mother and father at the two ends of a long table, five guests on each side and eight courses: Grapefruit, soup, fish, fowl, meat, salad, dessert and cheese, with potatoes, vegetables and the proper wines for each course. As we ate, two young Irish maids stood silently, one each side of a long table on a side wall, staring straight over our heads, in case my mother wanted anything. It seemed wrong to treat people like that but my own situation was not much better. I was expected to speak when I was spoken to, otherwise I watched and listened.

On other nights my mother and father would go to a ballroom in London, called the Empress Rooms, order a bottle of the widow (Veuve Cliquot champagne) and dance to the strict tempo of Victor Sylvester's band, but I stayed at home with the maids, which was nicer.

In the day time, my uncle Tom sometimes came by. He had a way with words, and once said "Beans are a noisy fruit" that stuck in my memory forever. And he told me stories of his life.

In the first world war he was a dispatch rider who carried messages on a motor-cycle and he claimed to have been to Belgium 250 times, because the front was in Belgium and the headquarters of his unit was in France, in an old chateau with a circular driveway that had a dry well in the middle of it.

Several times a day he would go there with messages and drop a grenade or other piece of explosive down the well, until it had a goodly number of them down there. Then one sunny afternoon when all the senior officers were having a nap, he pulled the pin out of a grenade, tossed it down the well and rode away.

Looking back, he saw a column of flame rise into the air, with the little hut from the well on top of it but he didn't stop to hear what the general had to say about it.

After the war, he was 20 and went round the world on five pounds (about 25 dollars then). First he stowed away on a ship, with the help of a seaman who opened up a coal bunker, put him inside and said he would open it later.

But as he sat there, in the pitch dark,

the coal began to go down and he realized he was on his way into the furnace, so he frantically twisted the nuts that held an iron plate on the other side of the bunker and took it off, to find himself looking into the funnel.

It was a ventilation shaft, about 20 feet across, with the exhaust pipe from the main engine glowing red in the middle of it and smaller pipes around the sides. There was a ladder going straight up it, too far away to reach, but rather than go down into the furnace, he leapt across and caught it. Then he climbed up to the top and looked down from the funnel.

There were men on deck, looking for something, until one of them pointed at him and said "There's the bastard". Then they made him wash dishes all the way to Australia.

There he was a Star Boarder in a boarding house, meaning he didn't have to pay any rent but had to sleep with the landlady, until one day he couldn't face it.

He knew he could never walk out with his gear, so he lowered it down into the street on a rope, went out empty handed, picked up his stuff and found a job as deckhand on another ship.

That took him to California where he had

a job teaching Spanish to the daughters of a Mexican rancher, because he spoke the high Spanish of Castille. He would ride over the hills behind Ventura with the two girls, on fine horses, all day but soon he tired of it and 'rode the rails' to Arizona - lying on the rails that were underneath a railroad car.

There he got a job as cook for some cowboys and was told that nobody wanted it. In fact, if anyone complained about the food, he was promptly made the cook. So he baked a pie full of horse manure, and the first man to bite into it said "My God, shit! But nicely cooked."

One night he was in a saloon in Tucson when some men came in and started shooting, so he dived under a table and watched the bottles behind the bar fly apart. It was all good fun until one man got hit by a bullet. He was not badly hurt but then they all calmed down and took him to a hospital.

When my uncle Tom was back in England, he got a sailboat he called a 'hooker' and used it mainly for 'birtling' - making love to young women. One day he sailed into Burnham on Crouch, a fancy yacht harbor on the winding river, with his girl friend, headed into the wind, lowered the sails and went below.

Lying in his bunk, he thought it was odd that boats kept going past so close and so quietly, until he went on deck and found he had frgotten to drop the anchor. They had birtled their way from one end of the harbor to the other, as the current swept their boat along, without hitting anything.

4. UP IN THE MOUNTAINS

One Christmas my aunt May - I called all my parents' friends uncle or aunt - arranged a trip to Switzerland for her son Colin and some others including me, to go skiing. We took a train from London to the coast, a ship across the English Channel, a night train across France, sleeping in our clothes, with our luggage on the floor between the two long seats and the cushions over it to make a communal bed, then a train up a winding valley and a cog railway that went steeply up to a small village high above, with no other way to get there in winter.

The village had two resort hotels, a church, a few shops and some houses, all on steeply sloping land. People went from place to place on luges (small high sleds) dragging them uphill, often with things on them, or riding them downhill quite fast.

The parson looked odd, all in black with a bible in one hand, whipping round a corner from one street to another.

The street signs were just a foot or two above the snow but in summer, when the snowmelted, they must have been very high. And most of the houses had two doors, one on the floor above the other, to be used in the winter and the summer.

Skiing was new then. There were no ready made skis. We went to a ski maker who checked our size and weight, asked whether we wanted oak or hickory and said "Come back tomorrow". They were as high as we could reach and the poles had big baskets on them, to use going uphill, for there were no lifts yet.

For the first few days, we would go sideways up a small hill one step at a time, then ski down toward our instructor, learning to steer and stop in a crude fashion. Then we would graduate to parallel turns and we were ready for the mountain.

At 5 am we were dressed and ready, when our instructor came to show us the way. There were no prepared trails, so we followed him up until about 1 pm, when we ate our sandwich lunches. Then he would lead us down, across open spaces, though woods, now and then sliding down a steep chute on our backsides, to the bottom. And at night we would dance Swiss waltzes in ski boots.

There were no ski patrols, or safety devices. We carried first aid kits, food, water and metal tips that we could attach to our skis if one of them were broken. I miss those days.

The next year, they had two big red toboggans, each holding a dozen people, on the beginners' slope. One was hauled up by a steel cable, while the other went back down. But we had nearly a hundred hours' skiing by then, so we climbed the mountain and came down by more interesting routes each time.

Skiing by moonlight was harder than we expected, because the light was so flat that we couldn't see the moguls, and in one place I went off a ledge about four feet high, into the air. The tips of my skis fell down into the snow and I went up in a great arc, the moon and stars whirling overhead, to land on my face. But the snow was deep and soft, so no harm was done.

The nuns from a nearby convent were allowed to ski but were required to wear their proper habit, so there were girls coming down some of the trails, each in a cloud of white cloth, somehow looking like sailing ships.

At 16 I passed the entrance exam for Oxford but did not go there. My father sent for me, gave me some money and told me to go to Europe to learn German and French, so I got addresses of people who took in boarders and headed for Austria, in nice time for the ski season.

There were no credit cards at that time and carrying cash would have been stupid, so I got a Letter of Credit from a bank, saying how much money they had of mine. When I needed some, I could present it with my passport to any bank, anywhere. They would give me what I wanted, cross out the total and show a new, smaller total on the Letter of Credit.

After saying goodbye to my mother and crossing the Channel, I took a train to Paris, then others across France and Germany to Bad Reichenhall, in the Bavarian Alps, on the border of Austria, where I stayed in a house with a few other foreigners but spent nearly all of my time in the mountains.

In the town was a square building and inside it was a red cable car, big enough for a dozen or more people to stand in, with windows on all sides. When everyone was aboard, a man slid the door shut and it went out through the roof.

The town dropped away below you and for a while you hung in space, between snow covered mountains, until the car slowed down and went up through the floor of the station at the top. Then you had a choice of ski trails and after a few weeks I was allowed to use the one that was reserved for the German army.

I made a picture of the start of that trail. It was parallel with the side of a hut in the background, meaning that the first hundred feet were vertical. Then you had to make a sharp left turn to avoid going over a precipice and off you went, down a narrow trail along the side of a mountain, with the snow rising high on your left and falling away on your right, more and more steeply, so that if you fell down, you would not stop.

One day I slipped off that trail and started sliding down toward a precipice, but luckily I was able to grab a small bush that halted my descent. Then lying in the snow, I worked my way to a point directly above it and started up toward the trail. That way, I was able to grab the same bush each time I slipped back, until I finally made it. I was alone, of course, so if I had gone over the precipice, nobody would know what happened until the snow melted and my body was found in the spring.

But otherwise it was a fine run, with glorious views, and later on the army men adopted me as a mascot, until the skiing season ended and I took a train to Munich.

That was a fine city. I stayed in a house near the English Garden, owned by a woman whose son Jurgen was the same age as me. She and her grownup friends were worried about the rise of Hitler and all that brought with it, but the young people saw only the flags, the bands and the fun. Many girls wore the brown shirts of the Hitler Youth, so Jurgen did too and I went along with him.

It was the time of the anschluss, when the German army took Austria, and Hitler came to Munich. We stood in the crowd as he marched down a street, a small man, staring straight ahead, with no sign of emotion, passing within 15 feet of us. Then we were in the Sportspalast when he made his famous speech.

It was at night. First there were bands and flags and men in uniforms marching up a hill, then three preliminary speakers to warm up the audience, then loud cheers as Hitler took the stand. In front of him was a button. When he pushed it, lights came on in several locations around the hall. And at each location, a group of his followers would cheer loudly, until the light went out, then obediently fall silent.

I still remember the opening of his speech: "Twenty years long" - applause - "have I worked" - applause, and so on, while we ate oranges and flirted with the girls and held up our right arms in salute as we shouted "Heil Hitler". It was a fine show and if any grownups were to object to it, they would risk being reported to the authorities by their teenagers.

When Hitler left, things calmed down and I made pictures of floodlit buildings, using a camera that I stuck to a wall with a big ball of putty and an exposure of several minutes, that came out very well, though they made the people in the shop where I had them developed and printed suspicious.

Munich was famous for its beer and the Hofbrauhaus was the place to go for it. In a huge basement there were rows of long tables, crowded with people, with a band on a stage at one end and everyone singing. You sat down anywhere you found a vacant place and a waitress would come up and say "Dark or light?"

Then she would give you a stein, with a piece of tape on it, fill it with the kind you had chosen and make a pencil mark on the tape. Any time you emptied the stein, it would be refilled by a passing waitress and another mark was put on your tape. If you didn't want any more, you left a quarter of an inch of beer in the stein and when you left, the total of the marks was your bill.

Munich was where I first made love to a girl. Walking back from the Hofbrauhaus quite late, I met a girl who made it clear she was available, so I followed her to her apartment, paid her modest fee and did what I thought I should. But nothing happened until she said "Sie mussen ficken" (you figure what that means) so I did and it all worked out.

By then my German was adequate, so it was time to move on. Saying goodbye to Jurgen and his mother, I took a train to Paris and moved into the house of Monsieur Vitry, a big man with a huge gray beard, and his wife who had a small black mustache.

They were friends of Monsieur Eiffel, designer of the tower, and very social. The day after I arrived, several men and women were sitting in the living room, drinking coffee and making small talk. I was next to a young woman and said to her in French "Did you have good skiing last winter?" but I got it wrong.

In German the word for `ski' sounds like `she' but in French it's like `ski' and `shier' means to shit. So my question caused quite a stir and even after everyone had been told that I was new at speaking French, I no longer felt really welcome.

So I left the house early each morning, took French lessons and strolled around the city, chatting with strangers, reading newspapers and learning the language until late in the evening, when I went quiely to bed. It worked quite well and in a couple of months I was ready to move on to another scene.

For that I chose Tregastel on the north coast of Brittany, a small seaside town, where I wandered along the beaches, talked to local fishermen and learned more French words, until the time came for me to go back home.

5. NORWAY & SWEDEN

In England you had to be 17 to drive a car but you could get a motorbike license at 16 and a three wheeler counted as a bike if it didn't have a reverse gear. So I bought an old Morgan for about 18 dollars. It had two seats, a pointed tail with one wheel inside it, a space for your feet where the engine might have been and, in front of the radiator, a twin cylinder engine.

The other two wheels were on each side of the engine and stuck out in front of it. There were no doors, the hand brake and the gear lever were outside and it had a tiny, useless windshield.

The brake pedal and the hand brake went to the back wheel, the other wheels had no brakes. It had two gears, one high and one low. To start the engine, you put a handle in the side of the body, but it was easier to push the car.

It wouldn't run, so I pushed it home, worked on it and a week later it was ready to try out. When I came to a crossroads, I tried both brakes but nothing happened. I'd forgotten to connect the cables. So I shot through the intersection, seeming to go faster but not hitting anything.

It was probably the most dangerous car ever built. If you brushed a curb, it would flip over. If you touched any brake on a slippery road, the car would spin around, out of control.

On a wet road, you had to stay close behind the car ahead. Then if he stopped suddenly, your front wheels would go up against his rear bumper and stop you safely but his car would shake and rattle, so you got out, picked up the back of the Morgan, turned it round, pushed it and got it going before he could catch you. But it was fun and I drove it all over southern England for years.

My father and mother separated and being without a car, she went to a shop and picked out a red one, an open four seater. She had got a driver's license years ago, before any test was required, and kept on renewing it, though she never drove any car.

So she had a friend show her how it worked and off she went. Far out in the country, she stopped at a gas station and paid an attendant to turn the car around. On the outskirts of London, she found a taxi and paid the driver to lead her home. And little by little, she became a perfectly adequate driver.

Then she saw an advertisement in a magazine saying that if you bought two first class tickets on a ship to Norway, your car would go there free, so she bought tickets for herself, my girl friend Joan and me.

When she bought the car, the dealer had told her to make monthly payments but now she got a letter from the maker saying 'We understand you intend to take our car abroad' so she was thoroughly insulted and paid the full amount.

Together we drove through Norway into Sweden, up beyond the Arctic Circle and down through Finland into Estonia, Latvia and Lithuania, all taking turns at the wheel, while I looked after the car's engine, brakes, tires and such.

In Norway I was standing alone on the grass a few feet from a precipice of a thousand feet or more, when a goat came over to see what I was up to. Not liking it, he decided to push me over, but I stood my ground and he contented himself with eating some of the cloth of my trouser leg and wandered off.

In Sweden we wanted mushrooms with our dinner but the girl waiting on us didn't understand, until I drew her a picture of one. Then she smiled happily and brought us an umbrella.

In Lithuania we rode across town in a two wheeled carriage with one seat, wide enough for three people, and a small one for the driver on a bracket behind it. The reins went over our heads and we could see forward on each side of the horse but when it raised its tail, we had to hold our noses.

From there we shipped the car back to England, rather than go any farther, because I had to go to work as a fitter in the factory where Ellams Duplicators were made. As the machines came down the production line, the girls who assembled them set aside any that wouldn't go together. Those we filed, hammered, sawed and bent until they worked as they should.

The social structure worried me. The son of a working man couldn't hope to rise beyond the rank of a foreman, in his whole life, which seemed unfair. But then my mother's maid said she wished she could be the maid of a travelling lady, and clearly that was the most she ever hoped for.

There were special cases, of course, like model girls. We had moved to London when I took my first one home for dinner and remarked on how nice she was, to which Mother replied "The virtuous model has yet to appear".

Another time, we were walking down a street when I pointed out a young girl in a mink coat, and she said "The young get their mink in the same way that the mink get their young".

She told me that when she was young, before the first war, gentlemen would take her to dinner in horse drawn cabs and if one of them didn't make a pass at her on the way to the restaurant, she figured her hat wasn't on straight.

Perhaps the English women of that time were different from those of today. An old lady who lived nearby was walking her dog along a foot path, between houses and a quiet road, one night when a man came out from behind a tree with a gun and said "Stick 'em up". Looking him up and down, she said "Stick what, young man, and up where?" And he ran away.

My Aunt Dorothy lived in the country and

bred Great Danes. One of her dogs grabbed someone's cat, but she was able to save it. However, a stranger saw the incident and reported it to the Society for the Prevention of Cruelty to Animals, so she was invited to a meeting and given a medal for saving the cat. She didn't have the nerve to tell them it was her dog, so she took the medal and left.

My father took up riding, so he bought a white mare, hired an instructor and went to Windsor Park, a vast area of grass and trees near Windsor Castle, with me following on a rented hack that tried to brush me off on trees, for I had no idea what to do, except hang on. Then it tried to mount the mare and he blamed me, though I had no control of the situation. But I wasn't invited again.

My Uncle Geoffrey was a serious rider. One day he was going over some jumps when his horse stopped and dug its front feet into the ground. He had a new top hat on and as he flew through the air, he took it off and held it in his hand as he landed on his head on the other side.

My father had been a pilot in the first world war, so when the civil war broke out in Spain, he flew an old biplane there. It had a top speed of sixty miles an hour and over the Pyrenees, an eagle came up to look him over, easily keeping up with him, until it got bored and wandered off.

After a while, I was sent to the factory in Watford, near London, where the supplies for Ellams Duplicators were made, and on weekends I did some sailing.

At Brightlingsea, a small port on the east coast, the railroad trains go out onto a pier, with the sea on three sides of it, and we were at a station near it when a woman called out to a porter "My man! Does this train stop at Brightlingsea?" and he said "Well, mum, there'll be an 'ell of a bloody mess if it don't."

One evening I was invited to dine with a very social family where I felt uncomfortable, and after eating a date, I couldn't find a way to get rid of the pit. But fortunately a curly haired poodle came by, so I put it on that.

In the summer of 1939 it was clear that a war was going to start, so I volunteered for the Air Force, then tried the Navy but they both found out I couldn't see with my left eye - I never could - so I went to the Armory, in Watford, and joined the Hertfordshire Yeomanry's 79th Regiment.

This time, in the eye test, I covered my left eye with my right hand, read the letters on the card, then covered my left eye with my left hand and did it again. Nobody noticed and my eyes were not checked again for seven years.

6 . DEFENDING LONDON

There was an atmosphere of people rushing around, doing things. The colonel showed me an old 3 inch anti aircraft gun, left over from the first war, and asked if I could figure how to work it. It looked simple enough, so I said "Yes" and he made me a second lieutenant. Another man had been a cook in a restaurant so he was made a sergeant. There was no time for tests. Off we went to defend London from an attack that would surely come in a few weeks, if not days.

I was given four guns, a predictor to aim them, a height finder and some tents, then sent to North Weald airdrome, east of London, which was one of the main bases for Spitfires and Hurricanes. The perimeter of the field was eight miles long and there were no runways. The airplanes were parked all around the edge, and when they took off, each one went straight across the middle, so there were plenty of close calls but they never had a collision.

The guns had wheels and could be towed by trucks but before firing them, we lowered them to the ground, took off the wheels and levelled them, setting them in a quadrant of a circle, with the command post at the center.

There was a height finder like a long telescope with a lens at each end and an eyepiece in the middle, with an operator who called out the height of an airplane, based on its range and angle of sight. Then there was a predictor, manned by four men, that was pointed at an airplane and figured from its movement how far ahead we should aim, to hit it.

Each gun had a crew of nine men to aim, load and fire it and there were other men to look after the trucks and run the camp. We built low walls of sandbags around the guns and the command post and waited for the party to start.

Every time we heard an airplane, we would all run out, take up our positions and aim at it. I had to decide whether to fire at it or not but since my eyesight was not good, I trained the height finder operator to call out "Target identified as frendly" and we would all go back to what we were doing.

That went on for quite a while, until one day he called out "Target identified as ... Christ, it's got crosses on it" so I said "Fire" to the sergeant and he shouted "FIRE" to the guns and his false teeth went over the wall, into a bush. Without hesitating, he called out "Number one gun, send a man to the command post" and set him looking for them while we fired at the airplane.

The noise of the guns was very loud and with four of them firing as fast as the men could load them, it took some getting used to. But the airplane changed course and after much shouting, we managed to stop them. Then the men replenished the ammunition in the gun pits and we waited for the next one.

In the early days of the war, our equipment was quite crude. Many of the soldiers guarding the south coast of England had nothing but bayonets mounted on pieces of iron pipe to use as spears. Our predictors were old and we seldom hit an airplane but often we seemed to frighten them away.

The Air Force pilots did much better. Most of them were 17 years old, though a few got in at 16 by pretending to be 17, and if they were alive by 19 they were made instructors because their reactions were too slow for that kind of fighting.

I ate with them when things were quiet. They always changed out of their flight suits into their uniforms for dinner. One time we were sitting around a long table with the Wing Commander at the head of it when a man came in, hesitated to disturb us, then quietly told him there was an enemy airplane approaching.

A young man on my left pushed away his plate, stood up and said "I've finished my dinner. I'll go and deal with it" to which the Wing Commander replied "Oh good. Thank you" and the conversation around the table continued, as the young man went off to fight the enemy, alone in the dark sky.

One of the pilots had a batman (an officer's servant) who was a communist and it seemed odd that the man had volunteered for that job. But he said "You're the comrade who flies the airplane and I'm the comrade who polishes the shoes, and that's all right with me".

Soon we were moved to a site farther east, where we could shoot at the airplanes sooner, and this time it was just a field of grass in the middle of nowhere. So I found a telephone that nobody was using in a red booth down the road and connected it to two of the wires on a nearby telephone pole, by baring a foot or so at the end of a piece of insulated wire, twisting it around a steel nut and throwing it over the wire. When it hit, the nut went round the wire several times, making a good connection, so that I had excellent telephone service in my tent.

The man whose line I tapped made a bit of a fuss, so when we left I gave his number to some local girls who were on the game and told them he was a likely customer.

The next thing we needed was heat. It was a cold winter and we had very little fuel for the stoves in our tents but there was a railroad line nearby, so I sent a man out there each day to throw rocks at the trains. The drivers replied by throwing lumps of coal at the men but they soon caught on to what we were doing and threw us some coal each time they went by.

Another good source of heat was a stack of railroad ties, about five feet high, that were laid neatly across each other. Every day we would pull one or two of them out of the stack, cut the ends off and put those back. That gave us a fine supply of wood that burned well because it was full of creosote. By the time we went, there were few whole ties left and the railroad men must have been surprised when they took off the top layer.

But we had to be careful with our supplies, so I had a man paint our heap of coal white, which he thought was weird, but it stopped people from taking it.

The men were all volunteers at that time and they behaved like civilians working together to get an urgent job done. Most of them were young and I knew more about engineering than they did, so I had no trouble controlling them. But one sergeant had some army background and when a man mentioned his testicles, I heard him say "Now you listen. Officers 'as testicles, sergeants 'as bollocks and you 'as plain balls".

Then the British Expeditionary Force was organized and we were ordered to defend the port of Le Havre, on the north coast of France. So we put the wheels on our guns, hitched them to our trucks and headed for Southampton.

7. LE HAVRE & ST NAZAIRE

The ship that took us across the English Channel docked in Le Havre right where we were supposed to be, so we took our guns off it and set them up nearby. Our Battery had three Sections, mine and two others, with a major in charge of them all and a captain as his adjutant. Between us, we were responsible for protecting the city and the docks from enemy bombers.

The attacks were sporadic. One or two planes would fly low overhead, dropping bombs here and there, then go away. It was virtually impossible to aim our heavy guns at them as they came in, so we fired at them going away. Our major, Peter Heber - Percy had no role in the action but there was a machine gun on a post for ground defence and he would spray the sky with bullets from that, a happy smile on his face, on principle.

One 3 inch gun was set up beside some big oil tanks, aimed up at an angle of 60 degrees and kept loaded. Bombardier (the equivalent of corporal in the artillery) King, who was not much good for anything else, was put in charge of it and stood there, day after day, by the brass firing handle.

Then down came a Dornier dive bomber, straight at the gun. King pulled the handle, the gun fired and down came the bomber, into the water. From then on he was called Dorniar King and treated by everyone as a minor hero.

Despite the bombing, life went on in the docks and the city, but with new values. I was sitting beside the driver of a truck, with bombs exploding ahead of us, when a man on a motorcycle came round a curve ahead very fast and hit the front of it. There was a sound like 'Clock' as his head broke wide open, and he lay in the road with his blood running down a drain. There was nothing we could do for him, so I told the driver to drive on and changed the conversation to take it off his mind.

We had enough men to let some off each night and they all went to the Rue de Gallons (Chevron Street) every time. It was a narrow road down by the docks, with no traffic through it, and each side was lined with brothels.

In fact they were full service bars where you could sit at a table, have a drink and maybe something to eat, listen to music, chat with your friends, and enjoy the company of scantily dressed girls who wandered by. If you wanted to have a brief affair with one, you paid an old woman at a cash register, at the foot of the stairs in a corner of the room, as you went up.

None of my men spoke French, so they missed some of the fun. A Scotsman in a kilt sat down at a table near me and three of the girls came over, giggling and chatting about what might be underneath it. Finally one of them lifted the kilt, looked under it, and said "Two balls and a banana" which they seemed to find disappointing.

Those places were licensed by the government, the girls were checked by doctors once a week, and the French thought the whole thing was safer and more sensible than any alternative. So in their way, they were quite respectable and the girls went out of their way to satisfy their regular customers.

But I was worried that my men might get venerial diseases, so I started checking around. I asked one man "Have you ever had the clap?" and he said "Have I had my breakfast!" with an obvious glow of pride. So I left it to the doctors.

When we left England, there were not enough doctors for our Battery, so they gave us a gynecologist and a veterinarian, which was quite good. The vet was more gentle with a needle than most doctors because, as he put it, "My patients can bite".

It did not take long for the German army to run the British Expeditionary Force out of France and when the evacuation started at Dunkirk, I was the only officer around who spoke French, so I was told to take my guns and 140 men about 200 miles across France to the port of St Nazaire on the Bay of Biscay.

About 30 of them were off duty when I got the order, so I took two sergeants to the Rue de Gallons and walked down the middle of it, while they went into the brothels on each side. In a few minutes we had gathered all of them, though I felt guilty about one man who had spent weeks getting up the nerve to take a girl upstairs and was on the first step when he was called back down and lost his chance forever.

We were on the north side of the Seine river, so we headed east and came to a ferry, a flat barge, that went across to the other side. A Frenchman was setting an explosive charge to sink it, but a British officer ahead of us put a gun to his head and convinced him to take us across first.

While we were waiting our turn to cross, a German bomber set some oil tanks on fire and the black smoke was so thick that the sky went dark and we had to use our headlights all that day, though it had been bright, sunny and clear.

When we were held up by the trucks ahead, one of my men got out to take a stroll and when he got back, we had left. So he waited until a tank came along, flagged it down and said "Let me in. The bloody huns are everywhere". A door opened and a voice said in English "We ARE the bloody huns".

He apologised, so they took his gun and made him sit on top of the tank, as they continued down the road. But later, when it slowed down, he jumped off it and luckily another British truck came along. It was that kind of day.

When we got to St Nazaire, we set up our guns and one of my sergeants came up to me, saluted and said "We have orders to stay here and hold back the Germans until everyone is on the ships", to which I replied "Jolly good, sergeant. That'll be fun". (Years later, he told me he remembered the exact words).

My guns had no sights for aiming at things on the ground, so we opened the breeches and peered down the barrels until we had two of them aimed down the road and the others aimed at places where a tank might come through, then loaded them and waited.

But I ran into a problem. There were abandoned trucks and motorcycles all around us and the sergeant wanted to set them on fire, to prevent the Germans from getting them. I hesitated because it seemed a waste, then told him to do it.

There were two British ships in the port, the Lancastria and Langefarach, large vessels with room for perhaps a thousand men in each, and the Lancastria was loaded first but a German bomber came over and sank her in the afternoon.

Many men were drowned but some were rescued and put on the Langefarach, with the rest of the men who were waiting. By evening they were all aboard, so we spiked our guns, joined them and the ship sailed, on the day that France surrendered to the Germans.

8. THE BATTLE OF BRITAIN

Next morning, the coast of England came out of the fog ahead of the ship and by noon we were safely in Plymouth. Then we were sent to a camp west of London, where there was nothing to do, but no one was allowed out of the gate. That was ridiculous. Most of my men had families in the London area, that had been bombed, and wanted to go and see how they were doing.

So I wrote out passes giving each of my men 10 days' leave, told my sergeant to have them parade in their best uniforms, with boots polished and brass shining, then I drew my sword, took my place at their head and marched toward the gate of the camp, with the sergeant behind them, calling out "Left, right, left, right. Pick 'em up there."

The man guarding the gate looked worried, hesitated, then up went the gate and he saluted as I went by, returning his salute and leading my men straight across the main road, into the woods on the other side, where I gave each one his pass and told him he was on his own for ten days. Good luck.

Then the sergeant and I went to the office of the colonel in charge of the camp and said we had sent our men on leave. Later, he told someone I was the only officer who did something for his men. All of them came back on time and, out of their meager pay, they collected enough to present me with two silver tankards engraved: For a Sporting Officer from the 140 NCO's and Men.

Soon we were sent to Blackpool, a seaside resort in northern England, where our regiment was being gathered. By that time, my father was commanding White Waltham airdrome, near Maidenhead, so he borrowed a Spitfire, took the eight guns out of the wings, put in his luggage and flew up to see me, staying in the clouds most of the way, although he had no blind flying instruments, to avoid being shot down by a passing Messerschmitt.

When most of the men in our regiment had found their way to Blackpool, it was given the job of guarding Swansea in Wales, that was a major port for the unloading of equipment and supplies arriving from the United States.

The golf club, on a beach a few miles from the town, kindly allowed us to use its club house as the headquarters for my Section, complete with a cellar full of Harvey's Bristol Cream Sherry available at a very modest price, so we pitched our tents around it and set up our guns.

Those were 3.7 inch ones, with shells twice as heavy as the old 3 inch guns, and a muzzle velocity as high as a rifle. The predictor was a new, more advanced model but the height finder was no better than our old one had been.

Soon the German bombers started coming in from the south at about 7 o'clock each night and we fired our guns until one in the morning, then carried fresh ammunition from bunkers to the gun pits, had breakfast and got some sleep, until a lone German airplane came over in the afternoon to look at the damage.

We had enough officers and men to let a few off each day, so we got to know some of the Welsh people. In many villages there were only a few surnames, so they added a person's occupation to identify him, like Evans the Meat or Reese the Coal. Once, I wanted to stop a man who was walking away, so I called out "Evans, Reese, Jones" and he looked back: "Sir?"

We were sent some models of German airplanes to put where our men could see them every day and learn to recognise them, so we found two telephone poles, painted them red, set them on each side of the road near the front gate, strung a wire between them and hung the Plane of the Day up there.

A few days later, a man from the phone company came looking for two poles that were missing. We told him we would let him know if we found them, and he never seemed to notice that we were standing between them as we spoke.

The nightly bombing of Swansea was confined to a small area around the docks, so when we had an evening off, we went dancing at a hotel on the other side of the town. My girl friend Eire (Snow in Welsh) looked elegant in evening dress, but when she said "My love wants you as much as your lust wants me" I thought it better to change partners.

Going back to the camp one night after the bombing was over, we found the tail end of a German bomb, so we took it to our Regimental Headquarters, and stuck it in the ground, next to the house, with an old alarm clock ticking inside it.

Next morning, they cordoned off the area, evacuated everyone and generally made a fuss until the bomb disposal people came and assured them that it was just a practical joke.

Later, they needed people for bomb disposal, so of course I volunteered - in a war, you do whatever is needed - and was sent for an introductory lesson on a hill outside Swansea.

The teacher arrived on a motorcycle with a bomb he had found bouncing in the sidecar, laid it on the ground with a small explosive charge beside it and led us away. It was early evening, before the blackout, and the lights of the city glowed like a great sea below the hill, until there was a loud bang and they all went out.

Evidently a cable bringing power to the city passed below that point and the explosion had disrupted it. So we applauded with enthusiasm and went back to our respective camps, never to hear anything about bomb disposal again.

Our Battery Commander, Major Peter Heber-Percy, was walking back to his camp one night after his car broke down, when a fire engine came up behind him, all lights and sirens, stopped and asked him where the fire was. So he said "That way" and got on it to lead them to his place, where he looked around and said "It must have gone out". They were suspicious but in a hurry, so they muttered things and went rushing off.

A merchant ship in the port had shot down two German planes with its one old gun, so all the officers of anti aircraft units in the area were gathered together to hear its Captain tell us how to do it. When we quieted down, he stood up and said "Fred's my gunner and he's a good wing shot. When I see a German airplane, I say to him: Fred, shoot the fucker down. And he shoots the fucker down".

The use of such words was encouraged by the army, probably as part of an effort to break down the men's natural reluctance to kill people, and it led to things with a certain charm, like the Wonga Wonga bird. When persued, it flies round in ever decreasing circles, finally disappearing up its own fundamental orifice, from which point of vantage it showers shit and derision on its baffled persuers.

To check our security, we made an identtity card with Hitler's picture, Goering's signature and DO NOT ALLOW WITHIN A MILE

OF ANY MILITARY ESTABLISHMENT on it. When we had someone from another unit show it to the man at our gate, he glanced at it, saluted and raised the pole to let him in.

A girls' school nearby was taken over by the Navy to house sailors. The first night they used it, bells rang in the lobby so the woman in charge went looking for the reason and found a notice in each bedroom saying 'If you require a mistress in the night please ring the bell' to which all of the sailors were responding with great enthusiasm.

The first anti aircraft Radar was sent to Swansea, with one of the men who designed it, and set up near my guns, so I spent my days helping him make it work.

It was in a trailer, about 12 feet long and 8 feet wide, mounted on a turntable. It had big, air cooled vacuum tubes that sent twenty thousand volts to two antennas, each several feet long, that we tuned by running our knuckles along, a few inches below them, and listening to the sound of the sparks coming down toward us, to find the nodes.

Radar was secret, so we called it GL (for Gun Laying equipment) and put it to work right away. We could measure the bearing and range of incoming bombers, so all the guns in the area could put up barrages in front of them. And we told the Air Force which way they were approaching.

That was so effective that we put out a story about our pilots eating carrots to improve their night vision, which had nothing whatever to do with the matter.

The Air Force people invited me to go up in a Blenheim, a twin engined bomber, to see things from their point of view. As I got in the plane, they took my parachute and told me to lie in the bomb aimer's position without it.

That was a plexiglass bubble in the floor, which would drop out if you touched that handle - I never knew which one - so I lay very still and tried to see what they were showing me, without much success.

About that time, I was required to attend a court martial. The plaintiff, an old sergeant, was the principal witness and he said "On Saturday the fifteenth of June, I was in my quarters, pleasuring my wife as is my wont on a Saturday afternoon, when 1945236 Gunner Smith, W. put his head through the window and said: Go it you randy old goat".

We asked the defendant if he said "Go it you randy old goat" and he admitted he had, so we found him guilty and convicted him of doing a thing that was contrary to the maintenance of good order and military discipline.

If we could make the Radar tell us the angle of sight of a target, we could figure its height and from that the ground range, which would be a great improvement. But the land around it was not level, so we pounded hundreds of iron stakes a few feet high into the ground and on them we laid a level mat of chicken wire to reflect the incoming signals up to the antennas. And soon we got better results.

In fact, Radar developed so quickly we were soon using a single antenna one centimeter long that rotated at high speed to give the effect of four antennas.

The Germans started bombing Cardiff, 35 miles east of us, so we moved to a site a few miles from the city, at a place called Bare Ass Bay. The land sloped down to the sea and at night the local lovers would be among the bushes, their white rear ends twinkling in the moonlight.

One afternoon a huge searchlight on a truck came by and its crew asked to stay the night, so we welcomed them and when it got dark we set up the light, pointing down toward the sea. Then we put loudspeakers half way down the slope, connected to an amplifier and a microphone.

At ten o'clock the searchlight people turned it on and one of our people started giving directions and advice over the audio system. There was much rushing around, hopping and flapping down below and a good time was had by all, with the possible exception of some of the people who were illuminated.

While in Wales, I visited a mine called Deep Navigation that was five thousand feet underground, where hard coal for ships was found. A few of us stepped into an elevator and the operator released a brake, letting us drop most of the way. The cage had sides but no front or back and the walls went past in a blur until he brought us to a stop at the bottom.

Then we walked over two miles through narrow tunnels to where men with pickaxes hacked coal from the vertical face. If there's a harder way to make a living, I don't want to know about it.

But the men sang. All Welsh people sang. On a bus complete strangers would sing in four part harmony. I once saw an old woman in a black dress and a tall, pointed hat like a witch get on a train with a harp. And a man on a bicycle overtook the train, as it went up a steep hill. Wales was special.

But the Germans had intensified their bombing of London, so we were sent to help stop it.

9. A HUNDRED WOMEN

As our forces built up, the cadre system developed. A few of our experienced men were called a cadre and put with a lot of new recruits, to create another unit. The Army tried adding a few women to a bunch of men, but that was a disaster. Then they tried an equal number of women and it worked very well.

My new unit had about 100 men from ship yards and 100 women from factories in the north of England, plus officers and NCO's of each sex. The men had razor blades sewn into the peaks of their caps, to slash people with. The women were as tough and I was their 21 year old commanding officer.

But it didn't take long to get control of that lot. In the world they came from, the real bosses were the old women. So all I had to do was look helpless and bat my eyelashes at the 5 female sergeants, and

I could get anything I wanted.

Technically I had no authority to punish anyone. All I could do was report them to the Major on his weekly visit. But we had a concrete tank about 20 feet square full of sewage, with a wall a foot high around the top and a big pump with a long handle that emptied it into a drain.

So if a man did something wrong, a sergeant would bring him to me and I would say "Do you want to be remanded for the Major or will you accept my award?." Every time, he would accept my award and I would say "Two days on the shit tank." Or maybe three days, if it was a serious offense.

Then each day he would stand on the tank, pumping hard to keep the stuff from coming up around his ankles. And usually he would not do the same thing again.

Meanwhile, the five female sergeants could think of things for the women to do, better than I could. And with equal num- numbers of men and women, the social structure they were used to soon devel- oped and quickly settled down.

The women called the sanitary napkins we gave them manhole covers and I thought some of them might not be very bright, so every night I sent a male and female NCO around the camp with flashlights, looking into dark corners. The ones who were smart enough to avoid my patrol didn't get pregnant and the ones who weren't smart enough got sent to bed, so it all worked out and nobody got pregnant.

We had to lay a telephone line to another unit, so I set out across country with some men, unrolling the insulated wire from a wooden reel, until we came to a river. So we took our clothes off, put them on the far bank and went back for the reel of wire. But there was a railroad track beside the river and when we were half way across, a train full of women and children, refugees from the bombing in London, stopped. That left us waist deep in cold water, with them waving and shouting at us, until after a long time the train slowly drew away.

Life in that camp went on as usual, firing our guns from 7 pm until 1 am then replenishing the ammunition - that was much heavier than the old 3 inch kind - in the gun pits, breakfast and some sleep, then odd jobs until the next evening.

I spent a day at a camouflage school and learned that you can hide in front of things, instead of behind them, if you look like them. And that people walking across a field of grass leave tracks that show up clearly in aerial photographs.

For some reason I was allowed to drive a tank. It was small and you steered it with two levers. When you pulled the left one half way back, it put out the clutch between the engine and the left track. When you pulled it all the way back, it put a brake on that track. And the same with the right lever. So on level ground, pulling a lever half way back would make the tank turn slowly and pulling it all the way back would make it turn quickly.

But we were on a series of steep little hills and when we went down them, using the engine as a brake, everything changed. Now pulling the left lever half way back made the tank turn right and pulling it all the way back made the tank turn left. And the right lever had the opposite effect, which was quite confusing.

Someone decided that all officers must learn to ride horses, so off we went to do that. Soon eight of us were trotting round in a circle, with stirrups crossed over the horses' necks and a sergeant in the middle. In those days a sergeant could say anything to an officer, so long as he said "Sir", and the man in front of me, Desmond Ashbrooke, was not doing too well. So the sergeant said "Leftenant, Lord Ashbrooke,

Sir. If Jesus Christ rode into Jerusalem on 'is donkey the way you're riding that there 'orse, No Wonder they crucified 'im.

Later, we were sent to the coast to practice firing at a red target, towed by an old biplane, with 3,000 feet of line between them. There was a loudspeaker on a pole near the command post, so that we could hear the comments of the pilot, and one of my men made a mistake, sending a shell in front of the airplane.

There was a loud CRUMP and a puff of black smoke. Then a voice from the loudspeaker said "Will you kindly inform the Director of Practice that I'm pulling this fucking target, not pushing it."

While we were there, we tried out a sight I had designed and built, to enable 3.7 inch anti aircraft guns to be used against low flying airplanes, which was not possible before. It did the job, and our Major had fun shooting at seagulls with it.

Then it was sent to the Ordnance Research Group and I heard nothing more until years later, when I was told it was called the Middle East Gun Sight and used against German tanks in North Africa. The 3.7 inch gun had a much larger shell and far more range than any gun a tank could carry, so it could easily destroy them.

Back at the camp, I filed incoming letters and memos in two boxes, marked SENSE and NONSENSE, which worked quite well until I went on leave, the Major went into my office and saw some of his memos in the NONSENSE file. When I returned, he told me life in the Army was an expendable asset and mine would not be worth much if I went on like that.

Our Regimental Commander was a Colonel of the old school, with gray hair, a neat mustache, high leather boots and a little cane that he slapped against them all the time. One day, he told me to go and measure a hut 30 miles away and the only transport available was a very big army truck, so I took that.

When I got there, I had forgotten to bring anything to measure the hut with but I had a poodle on a leash, so I used those and figured that I could convert the measurements to feet when I got back.

As I drove into the camp, the Colonel was standing there and he said "Well, how big is it?" I told him I didn't know yet, but he said "Don't be a damned fool. How big is it?" So I said "Well, sir, it's eight leashes and two poodles by five leashes, less a poodle." The effect was dramatic. He was so mad he couldn't speak and hopped up and down making a noise like a tea kettle, while I parked the truck and made my calculations.

I was not the only one to agravate him. Someone screwed his high boots to the floor, while he was asleep, and put a goodly dollop of syrup down inside them. In the morning, when he stepped into the first one, his foot forced the syrup up around his calf to create an airtight seal and he had to have a boot maker unpick it before he could go anywhere.

Then one day the General came for dinner. All the officers stood saluting as his car drove away, but it was parked with its rear bumper near the Colonel's tent, and someone had transferred some ropes from the tent pegs to the car's rear bumper. So the tent followed the car, which the General seemed to think was funny but the Colonel did not.

About that time, one of my men came and asked for four days' special leave. I asked what for and he said "Sir. My wife's been promoted to sergeant and I wish to fulfill a lifelong ambition." So of course I gave it to him.

Though our camp was about 40 miles from London, we could see the light of the fires in the night sky, as the Germans dropped bombs on it. But we had four days' leave every three months and that's where we went. That's where the action was.

With three months' pay to spend, an officer could eat and drink anywhere he liked, and meet girls who were out for some fun because they thought they might not live much longer. So it was easy to have a good time, and we did.

One morning I woke up in bed with an attractive blonde, but with no idea how I met her. At breakfast, she said "What's your name?" so I thought "Oh, dear, what have I done?" and gave her the name of my Major, Peter Heber-Percy.

As it turned out, she was a nice girl and we saw each other many times. To her and her friends, I was Peter and having got the name, I invented an identical twin brother called Peter whom I could blame for anything people disapproved of.

Gasoline for cars was rationed, so I bought an old one that was very cheap, but never drove it and put its gasoline in a motorcycle, a four cylinder Ariel, that had good acceleration but its engine had a habit of suddenly freezing up, due to inadequate cooling of the two rear cylinders. When that happened, the rear wheel would stop, the bike would go into a wild skid and throw the rider off, so I rode it with my left hand on the clutch.

Once I took a girl in evening dress to dinner at the Savoy Hotel, one of the fanciest in London, on the motorcycle. They had valet parking, so we gave it to a man and went inside.

When we came out there was a powdered flunkey in a white wig and knee breeches calling out "Lord Montagu's car" and things like that, so I gave him his tip and said "We require our motorcycle". Another man wheeled it up to us, managing to hold it as if it were a dead rat, then I started the engine and we swept out of there.

The Army bikes were BSA's and Nortons, with single cylinder engines. I was riding one down a country road at 50 or 60 miles an hour, when the ignition lead came off the spark plug and fell on the frame.

At once the whole bike was at high voltage, so I sort of hovered over it, trying not to touch any metal parts and coaxing it around curves by leaning that way until it slowed down and finally stopped.

Walking in London during the bombing, you made a note of any doorway, or other place, where you could shelter. Then when you heard a bomb coming down, you ran back to the last one, rather than go looking for one that might or might not be ahead. If there was no shelter within reach, you threw yourself in the gutter, and a girl I was with flipped her expensive fur coat around behind her, to save it from harm, as she did that.

By then, my mother was working for the Royal Dutch Military Mission, driving a General around London, and my father was still commanding White Waltham airdrome, where Amy Johnson was one of the ferry pilots for whom he was responsible.

On a typical English afternoon, it was raining lightly from clouds at 500 feet, but bright and clear above 4,000 so she took a Fairchild Auster, a 3 seater airplane, up to 12,000 feet, removed all her clothes and lay there sun bathing.

Maybe she dozed off, but she found herself in clouds and the airplane had no starter, so she went down through them. When she came out below them, she was about 300 feet above the ground, so she put the airplane down in the nearest field, and within minutes there were five farmers peering through the windows.

Father got a phone call saying there was a naked woman in a field, so he went to fetch her. Then he had to get the airplane back and fill out lots of forms. But later, he presided over the court of inquiry into her death. She was coming down from the north in thick clouds, with no blind flying instruments, so she went over the Thames Estuary and was feeling her way down, looking for the calm, smooth water, when she flew right into it

My uncle Tom was working as an engineer at the Royal Navy's Underwater Research Group and my old girl friend Joan was driving an ambulance. I met her one day, in a bar with her other driver, and after a few drinks, they said they should go. They had someone in the ambulance. I asked what was wrong with him, and they said he had been hit by an ambulance. Their ambulance. Which was why they were having drinks before taking him to the hospital.

Then a notice appeared on a board at our camp, saying: VOLUNTEERS ARE URGENTLY NEEDED TO DROP ALONE BY PARACHUTE BEHIND THE ENEMY LINES.

So of course I volunteered.

10. SPY SCHOOL

I got orders to report to an office in a big building in London, where I found one girl with a chair and a table in the middle of an empty room. When I gave her my name, she handed me a railroad ticket to Blandford, 100 miles to the southwest. That was all she could tell me, so I took the next train there. As I stood wondering what to do, a man came up and said "This way" so I followed him to a truck and off we went.

About ten miles down the road, he turned onto a secondary one, then swung into the driveway of a large estate. The gates were wide open and there was no sentry to be seen as we followed the winding road between high rhododendron bushes and came to a big, rambling old house.

Inside there were large rooms with ornate plastered walls, and wooden railings, about three feet high and a foot away, to protect them from damage, high decorated ceilings and bare wood floors, furnished with Army tables and beds.

There they taught burglary, forgery, silent killing, codes and cyphers, sabotage and the routine proceedures of espionage, all good stuff that might come in handy one day, plus of course the best ways to use knives, guns and garrotes.

The instructors were professionals. The burglar was one of the best, let out of prison to teach us, a short, quiet man who might have been a minor bureaucrat. He was forever after us for being sloppy in our work. When you blow a safe, the door should fall open. But as beginners, we would put a few more drops of nitroglicerine on the hinge, to be sure it worked. Then the door would fly across the room and we would get chewed out.

He was polite about it and though we were all officers of captain's rank in various services, we treated him with great respect and he taught us a lot. Go in through the front door of a house. Use a small crowbar, folded inside a newspaper. Never run away, walk. If you must run, laugh loudly so that people will think that whatever you are doing is in fun.

When you open a chest of drawers, start with the bottom drawer and leave them all open, it saves valuable time. Walk up the side of a stairway, so that the boards don't creak and warn someone that you're coming.

The forger who might have been a watch maker, frail and thin, with big ears, was forever bent over a table. He did beautiful work but you needed to be an artist to do the serious stuff. I couldn't hack it and settled for making easy things like passes, so I flunked that course, but they gave me a passing grade because I had a knack for silent killing.

The code and cypher man was a mad genius, interested only in letters and numbers, who taught us the importance of leaving two intentional errors in every message, one near the beginning and one toward the end, so that if we ever left one of them out, the people receiving it would know we were in trouble.

The espionage people were in from the field and bored with the dull duty. But the experts in killing, by knife or gun or garrote, were a cheerful, outgoing lot much given to practical jokes, so it was unwise to get into your bed without checking to see if anyone had wrapped explosive line round a couple of its legs, with a time pencil to set it off.

No one was ever canned for things like that, just as no Spitfire pilot was ever canned for flying under telephone wires. Those were the people they wanted. But one man was let go from the school when they found out he liked cricket. That was not the kind of person they wanted.

A psychiatrist came while I was there, to check the students out, but he didn't last two days. When he sat down with the first one, we had left his window open and three of us were crouched under the sill outside, taking notes. Then we held a conference and each of us gave exactly the same answer to every question he asked, until eventually he gave up.

There were about 20 students, though they came and went all the time, and they were from many different units, including French, Belgian, Dutch and American ones. But they all had common interests in sailing and skiing, so they may well have come from backgrounds like mine. And every one had a note on his records, saying 'This officer is unamenable to discipline'.

Life at the school was not easy. We were up at dawn, running across country before breakfast. There were classes all morning and after lunch we hit the obstacle course. That included a rope between two trees, fully 60 feet above the ground, that gave me the willies and a field of live mines that was no great comfort either. But somehow we all survived and slowly we got used to it.

For an hour each day, we fired guns (45 Colt automatics) from a crouched position at moving targets, and quite often we would be out half the night blowing things up. So sleep was the name of the game. Sleep and survival. In that order.

After a while, we were sent to parachute school, that gave us a break. When we arrived there, we were taken to see hundreds of men coming down out of the sky, looking happy, which was encouraging. Then a day of ground school, dangling from ropes and swinging around, and off to get our first parachutes.

The girl behind the counter said "If this one doesn't work, bring it back and we'll give you another" which she thought was funny, since we had no reserve chutes. Then there was a long line for the toilets, and off we went, to make our first jump, from a balloon.

Balloons were far more economical than

airplanes. You could put four men and an instructor in a square, shallow basket under a gas filled balloon, let it go up to 700 feet, have the men jump out and winch it back down, in a few minutes.

The 'basket' was a frame of steel tubes covered with cloth, about 8 feet across and a foot deep, with a hole in the middle to go down through, four jumpers sitting in the corners, and the instructor casually hopping from side to side.

Suddenly he said "All right, off you go" so I said "Me?" and he said "Yes" and off I went. The acceleration was 32 feet per second, so after four seconds I was doing about 120 miles an hour straight down, and my trousers were flapping in the wind.

With no forward motion, a parachute takes forever to develop and ours were operated by static lines, so there was nothing to do but wait for it to open.

Then things were pleasant, you could look around and hear dogs barking on the ground below. But almost at once it came rushing up, there was a bump and I was gathering up the parachute, feeling pleased with myself.

After that, we jumped out of American B-24 bombers. They had a gun turret underneath them behind the bomb bay, so we took it off and left a round hole to go through. In our business the bomb aimer figured the drift, lined up the airplane and let you know when to jump by turning on a light. If you faced forward, the air rushing past caught your feet and banged your nose on the side of the hole, so you faced the tail of the airplane and lay back on the wind to admire the plane going away.

One of us jumped too soon after the one ahead and found the other man's parachute coming up around him, before his own had opened, so he grabbed the cloth, held it tight and they both came down on the one, with no more problem than a broken ankle.

Since my left eye was no good, I wore a monocle, which was smaller and handier than glasses. And one does not wear a string on a monocle, so each time I jumped, the wind tore it away. But I had another in my pocket, that I put in my eye as soon as my parachute opened, so that I could land looking very British.

Not to be outdone, one of the Americans jumped with a cigar in his mouth, but somehow it went down inside his jump suit, he came down struggling to get it out.

Being British, we had fun with the Americans, like singing 'The Halls of Montezuma' to the tune of 'My Darling Clementine' (try it) but they saw notices in trains saying 'Please do not flush the toilet when the train is standing in a station' so they would sing "We believe in constipation when the train is in a station" to the tune of a children's song.

One day I saw an American on a bus trying to buy a ticket that cost a penny and a half - with the conductor standing over him, talking with a cockney accent - so I explained to him that in English that was a Tuppeny Ha'penny one.

The knives we learned to fight with were made like fencing swords, cut down to 12 inches long and named for our instructors Fairburn and Sykes. They showed us how to take a gun off a man but taught us that if you are faced with a man holding a knife properly, the best thing to do is go through the nearest window, without stopping to open it.

At that time no people except soldiers were allowed to go within five miles of the south coast, and one night we went down to a beach where the wreck of a ship was lying, to blow a piece off it with a necklace charge. We lit the two fuses and walked slowly to the shelter of a narrow trench.

There was a fine loud bang and when we

stuck our heads up, we saw a girl running down the moonlit beach pulling her blouse on, followed by a man with his pants round his knees, hopping like a kangaroo, with his shirt tails fluttering in the breeze, so we gave them a cheer.

The school was not unguarded. Game keepers with guns and dogs strolled around the estate, day and night, each with a heavy bag slung from his shoulder. One day I sneaked a look inside one. I found a radio, three hand grenades and some sort of black light. There was a machine gun in the rhododendrum bushes beside the driveway, and an airplane made a low pass over the area every few days, doubtless making photographs.

We learned other things, as time went on. Always fight to kill. Never use your fists. If you don't have a weapon, go for his balls. Meet in open places that are hard to bug and don't speak clearly. Mumble. Never do a job alone, have a look-out, preferably a girl. Grow a mustache to shave off and change your appearance. It won't leave a mark, you'll tan through it.

The Chief Instructor was a friendly, older man and he would take each student aside for a chat now and then. I must have mentioned that I had some experience in boats and knew the coast of France around Tregastel, because he sent for me and said "There's a vacancy in SOE that might suit you". And off I went to join the Special Operations Executive in London.

11. SPECIAL OPERATIONS

SOE was in a small building on Baker Street, that might have been a lawyer's office but there was no sign on the door. Inside, an old man sat on a high stool, silently staring over a newspaper. As I closed the door, he said "Your ID please", checked it, said "Upstairs, to your right" and went back to his paper.

There I met Roy Archibold, head of the Clandestine Communications Section, who worked for Colin Gubbins, head of SOE, who reported directly to Winston Churchill. So I paid attention and he told me everything I did would be Top Secret, even if I made a list of groceries to buy. I was now a civilian, paid out of secret funds, but I should wear my Captain's uniform when in England as cover, to avoid attracting attention.

I was to work with Jerry Holdsworth, who

was going across the English Channel in MGB's on moonless nights, to pick agents and airplane pilots up from the French coast. So off I went to Dartmouth, on the south coast of England.

That is a small port on a wide river, that narrows sharply to go between high cliffs to the sea, so it provided good shelter for the fleet of motor gunboats there. Those were like PT boats but with guns instead of torpedoes, and came in two sizes. The 68 footers were fast but if a wind came up out of the north, they had to slow down coming back from France and ran a risk of being out after dawn, sitting ducks for German fighters.

The 120 footers were slower but could keep on going in most weather, so we used those. There was an old ferry, a side-wheeler, anchored in the river as a mother ship, with MGB's tied up all around her and everything we needed aboard her, including repair facilities, cabins to sleep in and a good restaurant.

The MGB's were painted Mountbatten Pink, a pale red color that looked weird in the harbor but was almost invisible at sea in the late dusk or early dawn time. They had heavier guns fore and aft, lighter ones amidships, and were manned by the

Navy. We were just passengers, aboard them now and then.

The Skipper and crew were informal in roll neck sweaters and as soon as it was fully dark, they headed out to sea. There was a submarine net at the harbor mouth, with a narrow gap for the boats to go through, and the bow of ours touched the stern of the one ahead. At once a light flashed in Morse Code "If you do that again I shall scream". Then the Skipper took our boat up to her cruising speed of 20 knots and headed across the Channel toward the Triagoz Bank, a group of rocks and small, uninhabited islands off the coast of Brittany.

There was nothing there but the boat had short range radar and by going close to them, the Skipper could get a good fix of his position, after 100 miles of running in strong, variable cross currents before approaching the French coast.

There was a German gun position on every headland, sometimes as little as half a mile apart, and the best place to land was right under one, where a lookout would be least likely to expect us. So the Skipper stopped his engines one at a time, drifted into shallow water, and the crew lowered a small anchor to the bottom on a light line.

Next they launched a 16 foot double ended boat, with one man to steer and two men to row, using muffled oars, for the slightest sound might alert a sentry. Then there there would soon be searchlights on us and guns firing at us.

Jerry Holdsworth went in the small boat, landed and met one of our people, who had led four pilots and an agent to an exact point, each with a hand on the shoulder of the one ahead, as they walked in darkness along the beach.

Soon they arrived at the gunboat, came aboard and quietly went below, while the crew got the small boat on deck and the anchor up. Then the Skipper started one engine. The noise seemed sure to alert the Germans, but it didn't. And slowly we slid away from the coast.

Later I asked one of our French people about the noise when the engine started but he said it sounded like an airplane starting its engines, after gliding overhead, which was quite common and did not arouse any interest.

Clear of the coast, we resumed cruising speed, heading north toward England. Then the radar picked up two German 'R' boats, faster and better armed than ours, ahead of us. So the Skipper had some of his guns aim to port and others to starboard, went between the 'R' boats, fired a short burst and silenced them. Then we saw tracers arcing across the sky both ways, as the two boats fought it out.

On the way to Dartmouth, the agent gave us a roll of 35 mm film to take to London. He had been working for the Germans, building ramps to launch the first unmanned airplanes we called 'buzz bombs'. With that information, our Air Force was able to figure where their bases were and which way the launching ramps were aimed, so they knew what to prepare for.

One time we were on a beach when a light went on overhead and a German sentry came to the edge of a cliff. Two of us dived into the same bush and wound up facing each other, with water dripping off the leaves. He was taking a leak. So we waited for him to finish, and after a while the light went out.

Another time someone had the idea of leaving dummy lobsters full of explosive in the water for the French to pick up. So we went over there, cut open the sacks and dropped the contents into the sea.

Soon there was a howl of delight over the French radio. The lobsters were red, like cooked ones, instead of their natural black. But the German sentries didn't know any better, and the French fishermen carried baskets of them ashore.

Jerry invented the Holdsworth Box, a container that looked like a rock found along the Brittany coast. They could be filled with explosives and other good things and left on the shore for the fishermen to pick up. They came in different shapes and sizes, and blended in with the other rocks on the shore.

When a strong wind came up out of the north, even our big boats had to slow down, going back to England. Then we would break radio silence and ask for cover. At daybreak, a Spitfire would come out to circle overhead and protect us from German fighters. The boat was powered by four airplane engines, so we had a lot of gasoline fumes in the empty tanks and a burst of fire from a fighter would have blown us up.

The Non Moon Period only lasts three or four nights a month and the rest of the time I worked in London, doing odd jobs and learning the business. Clandestine Communications doesn't mean sending messages. It means moving things or people from place to place, without being noticed. You could call it smuggling.

One time, we were asked to get some watch movements (that is the works, without cases) from Switzerland for the Air Force, so we sent them to Gibraltar and gave them to the Navy, to take to England but the sailors pried the bottoms off the boxes and stole a lot of them. So next time we gave them to an existing smuggling organization and they all arrived safely.

Such organizations have been around for hundreds of years and we used them all the time for things that were not secret. A good way to send money to the French Resistance was to give a bag of commercial diamonds, dull gray stones, to a man in London and they would be where you told him two days later. The fee was ten percent of the value, and well worth it.

Money was not a problem, especially in France because we had unlimited supplies of francs, made in England by the same people who printed the pounds. They were excellent forgeries, aged and with good serial numbers. Usually we sent a million francs, which was about 14,000 American dollars, at a time.

We dropped the Dutch some carefully trained homing pigeons, to send us reports with, but all we got was a radio signal saying 'The birds are delicious. Send some more'. Then someone had to go and tell their trainer why they never came home.

There was a place called the Toy Shop, where happy geniuses made things for us to use. One of the best was a small mine, made to look like a piece of horse manure. On all the roads of France there were pieces of it every few yards, and such a mine was enough to break the track of a tank. So each time a German convoy came to a piece of horse manure, everything stopped and waited, while a man got out and poked it with a stick.

When the allied invasion started, the Second German Armored Division was in Pau near the Spanish border and it never did get to Normandy. When the tanks stopped at the horse manure, girls would entice the officers into the woods and kill them with knives. Children standing begging would put sugar in their gas tanks. It was a great success.

In peace time, Roy Archibald was an arbitrage operator. All day long he would sit in Paris, watching the prices of stocks on a ticker tape and talking on the phone to his partner in London. When the price of a stock was higher in one city than it was in the other, one of them would buy some shares, while the other one sold an equal number, and by the end of the day, they had both made some money.

He had a fine apartment with black silk sheets on the bed because his blonde girl friend looked good on them. When Paris was taken by the Germans, a Nazi officer used it but he kept it in good condition and eventually Roy got it back.

Before the war, Roy went to America on business but he had to go First Class on the ship, be seen in the best restaurants and stay in the best hotels everywhere, so all the money that he earned was gone by the time he got back.

Every job was different, but usually when there was one to be done, I would be told to meet a man at a restaurant for lunch. He would be a complete stranger, in civilian clothes, and would not say what it was about in the restaurant, because it might be bugged.

After lunch, he would take me for a walk in a park, and tell me what the problem was, like "We have two pilots in prison in Rennes, can you get them back?" That was a routine job, so I would get their names, go back to SOE and prepare a plan.

Then I would be given the key to a small

house, on a quiet street in London. Inside, there would be nothing - no furniture, no carpet - but a telephone with no dial on the floor. When I picked it up, a voice would ask what I wanted, and I would tell him we would need a B-24 on a certain night, give him details of the job and the coordinates of the drop zone.

One time I said "Could you put on a small air raid, a few miles away, to attract attention that way?" and the voice said "Certainly, sir. How many airplanes would you like and what kind of bombs do you prefer?" I didn't want to hurt anyone, just to make them look in that direction, so I asked for three airplanes and suggested they use incendiary bombs.

Getting people out of a French prison was easy. You took a room at a small hotel nearby, sat in the sidewalk cafe and handed out bribes - the money was no problem, it was fake - and after a while the men you wanted would be brought to you. Then you left town on bicycles, which were quiet and not registered, to go down to the coast and catch the next boat to England.

One time, a man came to us from the school and was going to drop into Belgium, when we found out he was a German spy. We didn't want to believe it, and checked very carefully, but it was true.

If we had held him back, the enemy would have guessed that we had found him out, so we let him go and fixed his parachute so that it didn't open. That's easy, you just cross one of the lines and it goes into a 'roman candle', unfolding to its full length but not opening. But it was a sad day. He was a brave man and it was hard not to think of him as one of us.

12 . WARTIME LONDON

Living in London, one got used to the nightly bombing, but I was surprised, one evening, to find the house where I was living had been hit in the daytime. One did not make a fuss about such a thing, but found another place and went on with one's life, glad to have the chance. Others were not so lucky.

But one's standards were different from those in peace time. A free evening meant looking for something interesting, and one thing I found was the Slip Inn. It was a club in a basement, run by an old lady of 40 and the certificate on a wall said that its purposes were 'Social and Sporting Intercourse'.

There was a dance floor with tables around it, a band and a kitchen. There were waiters, and a girl at each table, and they all paid the old lady for their pitches. The waiters sold food and drinks that they bought from the kitchen. The girls offered their services on a take home basis. The only people the old lady paid were the band and the landlord.

Of course I was fascinated by her and the way she ran her business. She didn't mind me sitting and chatting with her and I learned a lot. Technically, her place was a House of Assignation, so she had few problems with the authorities.

Now and then, a bureaucrat would close her down, but she knew a man who rented suitable places and got them ready ahead of time, in case anyone wanted them. So moving to a new place only took a few days and her regular clientele soon found it.

After a few visits, she started inviting me to her apartment at closing time - I was wearing my Army Captain's uniform - and told me it was her contribution to the War Effort.

At a party somewhere else, a haughty English woman was talking to an American officer about his ranch in Texas and asked how many acres he had. He said "About a hundred and fifty" and she said "That's not much" so he said "I'm sorry, ma'am, I meant a hundred and fifty thousand".

Another time, I went to pick up a girl at her apartment but she was not there. However her room mate was all dressed up and ready to go, so I took her out to dinner instead. And much later, I found out I had been exchanged for an old dress.

For some reason, I had to read the lesson in a church about 30 miles from London one Sunday, so I hopped out of bed without waking my girl friend, went out there, put on my dress uniform, unsheathed my sword and led some men to the church.

I like reading the Bible aloud, because it has such a fine sound, like "He said unto him Go. And he Went". So I put on a good show, led the men to their camp and went back to London. My girl friend was still asleep, so I slipped quietly into bed, without her knowing I had left.

But others were not so lucky. My friend Colin in my early years was a clean cut, enthusiastic type who wanted to join the Canadian Mounted Police. When the war started, he volunteered for the Air Force and became a Mustang pilot, sent on 'train busting' missions over France.

That meant he would dive down on trains full of people and kill them with his eight machine guns, which he did, as he was told. But to the people in the train, he was an evil man, and one day he was shot down in flames by a German fighter, to the cheers of the passengers.

My father was transferred from White Waltham airdrome to the Ministry of Aircraft Production in London. The carpet in his new office was old and ratty, so he had a nicer one installed. Then a man put his head in the door, muttered something and went away. The next day, all the furniture in his office was taken away and replaced by much bigger and better things.

It turned out that the carpet in a man's office was an indication of his rank. Father's job was a new one, just created, and he had raised his rank by several degrees.

But his Income Tax was something else. One year, he had to pay Income Tax plus Surtax and Super Tax, which came to more than a hundred percent of his income for that year.

One day at SOE, I said to an older man "What would happen if the Germans invaded and took England?" and he said "Within three weeks, you and I would be wearing new uniforms and doing the same things that we are now" which struck me as being somewhat less than patriotic.

For a while, France was divided into two

parts, the northern part being occupied by Germany, while the southern part remained under French control. So some of our people built a raft of metal drums and wood, inside the water tank of a steam locomotive. Then a man could climb inside the tank, get on the raft and go all the way to Paris, without the Germans suspecting he was there.

The railroad men were often Communists and some of the most reliable members of the French Resistance, as well as being the best organized, so we were glad to work with them, even though we doubted their political views.

When you parachuted into France, they would often be the Reception Committee at the drop zone. They would dig holes to bury the parachutes, dispose of unwanted earth, keep the sod to replace, then hold up three white lights and one red one. The three whites told the airplane which way the wind was blowing and the red one indicated the downwind end.

When the people landed, the Reception Committee would bury their parachutes, give them bicycles and lead them away to a safe house, where they could rest up and get organized. But when we sent money to them, they would often radio "Missed that lot. Try again" and a few days later a pissed off B-24 crew would dutifully go back and drop them some more.

Once I arrived back with three large suitcases, took a taxi to a building in London and dumped them on a wide sidewalk with people walking along it, while I carried one at a time up to an office. Later I was told the contents were worth a quarter of a million pounds - about a million dollars - each but no one had said that. And what was in them I shall never know.

A month before the allies invaded Normandy, we had to stop operating on the coast of Brittany, so I was told to go and help Vic run his smuggling organization out of Lyons in France.

13 . THE SWISS BORDER

When I arrived in Lyons, Vic said "You're a new boy, out of the school, aren't you? Well do me a favor, kindly refrain from leaving a trail of dead bodies across the countryside that leads to me". He was middle aged, stocky and used a job as an insurance agent as cover for his other activities. He had parachuted into France three times and built up an organization that took people back to England, mostly by walking over the Pyrenees into Spain, by way of the tiny state of Andorra.

Now he was working the Swiss border and I was to be his lieutenant for that. Neither of us knew where the other slept. That could lead to a visit by the Gestapo in the middle of the night, if the other one were caught and tortured. But we met each day at a coffee shop by the railroad station.

The first thing he noticed was that the knot of my necktie was too tight. An Englishman wears it that way, but a Frenchman ties it more loosely. That was a bad mistake - I hadn't worn a tie in France before - and I could easily have been caught.

Vic had an imaginary lieutenant in Paris. The people working for him in Lyons reported to an office in Paris but the man there was just a stooge who relayed the messages back to Vic, who was watching them go about their work in Lyons.

An organization like that usually had three men, the leader, his lieutenant and a radio operator, plus about nine girls. Our radio op was Jacques, who had several sets in suitcases that the girls moved to a new location after each transmission.

Girls were less likely to be stopped and searched than men but they put other things in the suitcases with the radio sets. One had hers full of chocolates and a German took a handful out of it, without getting down to the radio.

Our radio sets were rather crude. You had to plug one into an electric outlet and string a wire antenna around the room before using it. And even a man good at Morse Code took a while to send a message which gave the enemy a chance to use their direction finders and locate him. So Jacques kept a gun handy to fight it out, in case he looked like getting captured.

The Germans had better radios, where they could record a message on a tape, then go on the air and play it back quickly, but ours did the job and they were reliable.

One thing Jacques liked about his job was that when radio operators were trained in England, they were encouraged to have affairs with the girls who would be receiving their messages. Then later, when the operator was in the field, the girl could tell by his 'fist' if he was in trouble.

We were all taught to send messages in Morse Code with a key, in case we ever needed to. I had trouble sending at 22 words a minute, which was far too slow. But I was good at spotting radio antennas on roofs.

If you told England there was a half wave dipole of a certain length on a building, they could figure the frequency, and from that they could identify it, as headquarters of a German division, or whatever.

When I was at SOE in London, we knew of

1,200 German agents who were in England at one time. If we had picked them up, they would have been replaced and we would have had to find the new ones, so we kept an eye on them, and fed them false information. Now that I was in France it was spooky to wonder if one had been identified, and was being watched like that.

My car was a black Citren 11 (light) that anyone might have and one of my first jobs was to go to Annemasse and pick up a man who had come from Italy into Switzerland. He said he wanted to join our organization but Vic thought he might be a German agent trying to penetrate it. So he told me to take a gun. I took my Colt 45, cocked it, made sure the safety was off and put it in the glove compartment of the car.

When I got to Annemasse I realized that I had not asked Vic how to find the man, so I bought a bag of small red apples and sat in the gravel square in the center of town eating them. Of course Vic had told him how to find me and about the third apple he got in my car.

We drove over the mountains to Lyons, stopping at a restaurant for dinner and each politely insisting on paying the bill. Then I handed him over to Vic, and never knew what happened to him.

It was typical of that work that you saw a small part of a thing, without knowing (or enquiring) about what came before or after it. My gun was in the glove compartment, in front of the man, so he could easily have used it on me, but more likely he would be out to catch someone more important. Still, I put the gun away and never took it with me again.

The whole idea was to conform. I dressed and spoke like the people around me, my underwear had French labels, and after a while, I would dream in French. I had two code names, Grandmother and The Small Cigarette Lighter, and tried to do what was needed with as little fuss as possible.

One day I was having a picnic with a girl on a grassy hill, when she offered me a piece of candy, and I saw an 'L' tablet in the paper bag, among other things. It contained potassium cyanide and we all had one, to bite onto if we wanted to die quickly. The German ones were different, so she wasn't working for them. And she wasn't working for us, so she must have been working for Naval Intelligence.

By the way, a good place to leave a message is taped behind the water tank in a public toilet. And a dry cleaning shop is a fine place for clandestine operations. People can come and go, carrying things, without attracting attention.

The Citroen 11 was interesting. It came in three sizes with the same engine, so you could have a large, slow car or a small, fast one, depending on your needs. In any case, it had front wheel drive and if anything went wrong, they undid four bolts and took off the engine, gearbox and two front wheels. Then they lent you another set, while they fixed yours.

A scientist from Cambridge University was sent to us, to be taken into Switzerland to meet an agent who had just come out of Germany. No one should know about his visit, so I drove him to the border and slipped him through a gap in the fence, while girls working for us kept the Swiss guards busy, to the left and right of it. Then I took him to Bern.

We met the agent in a coffee shop, which was fun because two men at the next table, a German and a Japanese, were talking in their only common language, which was English. Then the scientist and the agent went for a walk in a park, while I followed at a discreet distance. And when they finished, I took the scientist back, through the border, to Lyons.

That night, he was very disturbed and told me there was a new kind of bomb, so powerful that five of them could wipe out London, and the agent had found a factory being built in Germany to make them. So I got him back to England and the Air Force bombed it, before it was protected.

That was the Atom Bomb. Some of our people had destroyed the German plutonium plant in Norway, but there were about twenty tons of it made, that were put on a ferry to go to Denmark, and one of our people was sent to stop it.

In an ordinary kyak, he paddled across the harbor in Norway to the ferry boat at night, with a limpet mine - the size of a large book, with magnets on it - but it wouldn't stick on the hull because of the barnacles. So he got out a pen knife and started scraping them off.

A head came out of a porthole above him and said something in Norwegian, so he said "Ya, ya" and went on scraping. Then the mine adhered, and half way between Norway and Denmark the ferry boat sank. So it only took a dozen people to finally stop Hitler from getting the atom bomb.

The British Consul in Bern spent a lot of his time driving around, doing jobs for intelligence people, as all consuls do, but he was only allowed a few gallons of gasoline each month for his car, so one day he said "You're in the smuggling business, smuggle me some petrol" which seemed reasonable.

Vic borrowed a bowser - a big truck, of the kind that fills up gas stations - and I drove it to the Swiss border, where I gave a man some fine fake papers we had made. He looked up and said "Is this your truck?" and I said "No, thank God" and he let me through. Nobody stops a thing that big.

The Consul's office was on the second floor of a building in Bern, so I parked in front, went upstairs and said "I've brought your petrol, sir". He said "Oh, thank you" then, not seeing a can, he said "Where is it?" and I said "Outside".

He looked out of the window, saw the truck and said "Christ. Get that thing away from my office" so I took it to a farm where they had a big underground tank and filled it up for him to use.

Before going back, I had 18 new tires, plus two spares, put on the truck, that were worth a lot in France, because there were none to be found there. So I made some spending money, and Vic didn't mind. It was all part of the game.

After France was liberated, I was at a

party at the Consulate when a rat faced little man came up beside me and asked what my religion was. So I said "Agnostic" and he spun me round to face a Bishop in full regalia - all red, with a big hat - and left me to defend my position against a professional.

Someone suggested that I might like a Job as a Vice Consul, then told me about one who was sent out to a remote island in the South Pacific, where he was expected to help the natives catch octopuses.

He had to dive down, let an octopus grip him in its tentacles, then wait for the men to bring the whole thing up to the surface. But somehow the idea didn't appeal to me, so I gave up the idea of going into the Consular Service.

With things so quiet, I took a girl for a ski vacation in the French alps and she was good at everything. But she was the only girl I remember who demanded that I make love to her when she wanted it, in a loud, clear voice.

When the war in Europe ended, we borrowed a truck from the Air Force to carry our personal belongings, including 140 cases of Martell brandy, and went up to Paris to celebrate.

There I was asked to defend someone in

a Court Martial. The charge was that he was seen running through the streets of Paris, with no clothes on, chasing a naked woman. So we looked up the Regulations and found one that said `An officer must wear the proper uniform at all times, except when engaged in a sport, in which case he may wear the clothes appropriate to the sport in which he is engaged.' So we showed that to the Court and they agreed that he had not done anything wrong.

14. CEYLON & SINGAPORE

Back in England, the war was over, but at SOE I was told to pack my bags and go to Ceylon (now Sri Lanka) right away. A plane was ready to take a dozen of us. It could not go that far in one flight, so they had air crews standing by at Malta and Karachi. When we landed, they refuelled the plane and the next crew took over, so we got there in a couple of days.

They were preparing to invade Singapore. The Allies were to land on the beaches while Force 136 would go in behind, leaving the Japanese between them. My job was to drop in by parachute and make sure the wrong people didn't shoot the wrong people. How I was supposed to do that was never clear to me, but they said it needed doing and I assumed they were right.

If you saw the film 'The Bridge on the River Kwai' you may remember the song they sang. Now here are the words:

Hitler - Has only got one ball.
Goering - Has two but very small.
Himmler - Is somewhat similar.
And Goebbels has no balls at all.

Try singing it and you can tell it fits the tune exactly.

The last minute planning was being done at Kandy, up in the central mountains, which was cool and pleasant after the sticky heat of Colombo. Every day, I walked up a hill from my house to the office. And half way up the road, there would be a pile of horse manure, big enough to fill a wheel barrow.

It was something of a mystery, until I found out that an elephent lived with his master at the bottom of the hill and worked in a lumber yard near the top, picking up logs with his trunk and moving them from one place to another.

There was little for me to do until the show started, so I borrowed a small open sailboat, took it on a truck to Trincomalee on the northeast side of Ceylon and sailed it about three hundred miles down the coast to Galle on the southwest side.

Every morning, we had to swallow quinine

pills at breakfast, to guard us against malaria, and they tasted horrible. Then we discovered they could be dissolved in gin, so we did that and served the resulting liquid with tonic water, before dinner, thereby creating the famous Gin & Tonic.

When the atom bombs were dropped and the war ended, the Navy put on a celebration in Trincomalee, a big, wide harbor full of ships. Among other things, there was a destroyer tied up to a dock, with a torpedo facing out over the water.

An old lady asked a sailor how they fired it and he said "Like this, ma'am" and pulled a brass handle. The torpedo jumped out of the launcher into the water, went across the harbor and sank a ship on the other side, which caused quite a fuss.

About that time, we got news from Singapore. Instead of going into the harbor, the Allies decided to land on the beaches as they had planned. But someone got the tide tables wrong and half the ships were stuck on rocks or sand bars, with Japanese tugboats pulling them off, which was embarrassing.

There was nothing more for us to do in Ceylon so we went to Singapore to tidy up the loose ends and I stayed in a chummery. That was a nice house, with a grass lawn running down to a beach, shared by six officers. Each month, one of us would take charge, tell the cook what to serve, pay the staff and bills, then divide the cost equally between us. It's a fine scheme.

There was a parade, with bands and flags, and Mountbatten's wife turned up with Air Force blue hair. Then he made a speech in Chinese but we weren't sure how it would sound, so we led wires from his microphone down to a Chinaman, under the podium, who said it again.

At sea level, almost on the Equator, it was hot and damp. I left a pair of polished brown shoes under my bed and by morning they were covered with mildew. Standing in a stone cathedral at midnight, the sweat poured down our faces.

So I went out to the airport, found four leading edge fuel tanks from old airplanes and built a catamaran. Each tank was 12 feet long, narrow and U-shaped, with one flat side. Welding two of them together made a 24 foot hull, and on the two hulls we built a wooden platform, then added a mast and a home made sail.

Offshore, there was a good wind and she went quite fast, with space for people to eat, drink and sunbathe. We used an oar to aim her, then she would go straight until we changed course.

But one day I lent her to someone who ran into the local pirates. They killed him and his friends for their watches and money. The bodies were found the next day.

I had a batman in Singapore who spoke Pidgin English, a language developed by sailors long ago, using English words and Chinese grammar. One day he was looking sad, so I said "What's wrong?" and he said "Me got altogether mary too much". He was having woman trouble.

With the heat and the damp, we tended to have problems on the skin between our legs. Then we would go to a doctor whose house faced a grassy lawn surrounded by trees. He would open two big glass doors, apply an ointment and watch his patient go running around on the grass.

There came a time when there was no more to do but wait to go home, so I went to the town dump and found a Type 100 Fiat, a racing car with no doors and a long pointed tail, being used to haul things around a yard. So I bought it for very little, took off the tow hook and painted it blue, with a brush.

It had two seats, side by side, with the driver's slightly ahead of the other one. The brake and gear lever were outside and you started it with a handle at the front. After trying it out I set out with a friend to drive through Malaya and up into the mountains to Kuala Lumpur.

We followed a causeway, with the sea on both sides, then the road headed inland, with little to see but trees. The car ran well and that evening we came to a rest house (the equivalent to today's motel) a low building with a veranda.

Other people were there and we were sitting having drinks when a waiter asked if we would like chicken for dinner. We all agreed it would be fine and a few minutes later, a scrawny old bird went running across the lawn in front of us, followed by a Chinaman with a hatchet.

One of the men with us suddenly picked up a glass and put it down on the table over a beetle. He was an expert in such things and said it was a new species, not known before. A woman called Mary Adams was sitting there, so he named it the Mary Adams Beetle.

The next day we reached Kuala Lumpur, a beautiful city, high in the mountains, with wide avenues and white buildings, shining in the sunlight. But by then, the time had come to drive back to Singapore, and board a ship for England.

As she steamed across the Indian Ocean toward the Suez Canal, I realized that my seven years in the Army were coming to an end. Gone were the days of taking risks to get things done that needed doing, of being a part, however small, of something big and exciting. I was 26 years old and that part of my life was ending, some of it to remain secret for many years.

Ahead lay the prospect of working from nine to five in the family business, virtuous, profitable and dull. But I should give it a try.

CPSIA information can be obtained
at www.ICGtesting.com
Printed in the USA
FSOW01n0745190515
7249FS

9 781450 212571